Bradwell's Pocket Walking Guides

Essex

BRADWELL
BOOKS

Published by Bradwell Books

9 Orgreave Close Sheffield S13 9NP

Email: books@bradwellbooks.co.uk

British Library Cataloguing in Publication Data: a catalogue record for this book is available from the British Library.

1st Edition

ISBN: 9781910551929

Extracts edited by: Louise Maskill

Design, typesetting and mapping: Mark Titterton

Photograph credits: VisitEssex.com - Front Cover

Print: Gomer Press, Llandysul, Ceredigion SA44 4JL To Be confirmed

CONTENTS

FACT FILE

The information in the walk descriptions is produced in good faith, and should be adequate to get you from start to finish, but it is always advisable to take a relevant Ordnance Survey map with you. The correct maps for each walk are recommended in 'The Essentials' sections – OS Explorer maps are highly detailed maps of a relatively small area (1:25,000 scale, 4cm on the map equals 1km on the ground), while the OS Landranger series are less detailed (1:50,000 scale, 2cm on the map equals 1km on the ground) but show a larger area per map. For these walks the Landranger maps are adequate, but the Explorer maps are more precise – the choice is yours.

All the walks in this book follow rights of way or paths open to the public, with occasional roadside paths (take care when crossing roads). The walks should be suitable for most people, especially families, ranging in length from around 3 to 6 miles. They are graded and described in 'The Essentials' sections to help you select the most appropriate walk for your party. Walking boots are recommended for all walks, with plenty of insulating layers of clothing and a waterproof jacket and over trousers if indicated by the weather forecast.

Locations for purchasing refreshments are suggested in 'The Essentials' sections, but are usually located at the start and end points of the walks, so packing a drink and a snack for your walk is advisable. Take advantage of public toilets where available!

By law, dogs must be kept on a lead wherever there is livestock, as well as in moorland areas during nesting season and where sheep roam freely. They should also be on a lead if they are likely to be a nuisance to other walkers or cyclists, and certainly when crossing roads. **You should be sure that your dog can manage to get over stiles before you set off on any of these walks; see 'Route' in 'The Essentials' to check whether there are any stiles on the walk you would like to undertake.**

Bradwell Books and the author have made all reasonable efforts to ensure that the details are correct at the time of publication. Bradwell Books and the author cannot accept responsibility for any changes that have taken place subsequent to the book being published. It is the responsibility of individuals undertaking any of the walks listed in this book to exercise due care and consideration for their own health and wellbeing and that of others in their party. The walks in this book are not especially strenuous, but individuals taking part should ensure they are fit and well before setting off.

INTRODUCTION

On first impression the county of Essex seems to divide neatly into two halves: the crowded suburban south with its busy industrial towns along the Thames Estuary and neat ranks of modern housing stretching out of sight; and the empty and agricultural rural north, with little villages reached by narrow lanes, half-timbered houses sprawling around a village green. In reality there are some beautiful parts of the county in the south. To the east the land is very flat, with endless mud flats and salt marshes – a paradise for birdwatchers and nature lovers.

This book scratches the surface of the walking routes in the county. Epping Forest features in only one walk, but there are plenty more paths and tracks to discover. Other areas worth exploring are Thorndon Country Park near Brentwood, Danbury Common and village near Chelmsford, and Dedham Vale along the River Stour on the border with Suffolk.

Colchester's proud boast is that it is the oldest town in England. The settlement was founded towards the end of the Iron Age, not long before the arrival of the Romans in AD 43. Later the town became Camulodunum, a *colonia* or centre for retired soldiers, bringing Roman culture to the area. After the death of the Emperor Claudius in AD 54 he was deified and a magnificent temple was built in the town to worship him; its centrepiece was a lifesize bronze statue.

The Roman fort of Caesaromagus was at the confluence of the rivers Can and Chelmer. The settlement's name became Ceolmaer's Ford in Saxon times and Celmeresfort in the Domesday Book. By the end of the twelfth century, after the building of a bridge and the granting of a Royal Charter giving permission to hold a market, the town had become Chelmsford.

The complacency of the Roman settlers was shattered in AD 61 when King Prasutagus of the Iceni died and left his widow and their two daughters in the care of the Roman Empire. Boudicca and the Iceni led a popular revolt against Rome, destroying Colchester and burning the survivors alive in Claudius's temple. The bronze statue was smashed, but amazingly the severed head was found in 1907 by a boy swimming in the River Alde in Suffolk; it can still be seen in the British Museum. Boudicca and her army went on to destroy London and St Albans before being massacred by a Roman army.

Every village in the county seems to have its own derelict World War II airfield, and the county is also well provided with Local Nature Reserves (LNRs) and Sites of Special Scientific Interest (SSSIs). The Essex Wildlife Trust looks after nine visitor centres, two nature parks and eighty-seven local nature reserves.

1. CABBAGE WOOD

THE ESSENTIALS

Distance: 6 miles (9.6 km)

Route: Easy, several gradual slopes, some stiles and gates

Time: Approx. 3 hours

Terrain: Hard tracks, grassy fields, field edges and wider hardcore farm roads

Starting Point: the corner of High Street and Station Road, Newport. Grid ref TL 521337, postcode CB11 3PL

Parking: Sensible roadside parking in the village

Food and Toilets: The Coach and Horses, Cambridge Road (CB11 3TR). No public toilets in the village

Maps: OS Explorer 195 (Braintree and Saffron Walden); OS Landranger 154 (Cambridge and Newmarket) and 167 (Chelmsford)

INTRODUCTION

Most of Debden Water, on your right during the first half of the walk, is a Site of Special Scientific Interest. Debden Water flows east to join the River Cam, while not far away at Debden Green is the source of the River Chelmer flowing in the opposite direction.

Before the construction of the M11 motorway the road through Newport was the A11, carrying a large amount of traffic because it was the main route from London to Norwich. A toll was once charged for crossing the bridge at the northern end of the village; a noticeboard on the Toll House Bed and Breakfast gives a list of the charges that were levied.

Debden Hall was purchased by Richard Chiswell in the early eighteenth century and rebuilt by the architect Henry Holland in 1795. At the turn of the nineteenth century it was owned by the financier, industrialist and politician the 1st Baron Strathcona and Mount Royal. His daughter the 2nd Baroness inherited on his death, but the hall was considered too expensive to run and it descended into decay. It was demolished in 1936.

Newport High Street is full of interesting buildings; Monk's Barn is probably the most remarkable. It is a typical Wealden house, so-called because the design is most often found in the Weald of Kent. The house is timber-framed with four bays, the two middle ones making a hall open to the roof with a central fireplace. Early houses had thatched roofs and wattle-and-daub walls; later examples became more sophisticated with overhanging jetties on the first floor, tiled roofs and brick infilling to the walls. Monk's Barn has a brick infill in a herringbone pattern.

The railway line through Newport Station is the West Anglia Main Line from London Liverpool Street to Cambridge and King's Lynn. Permission for the line was given by Parliament to the Northern and Eastern Company in 1836, but by 1843 they had only managed to reach Bishop's Stortford. Eastern Counties Railways took over the operations and soon got things moving, and the line to Cambridge and Norwich was opened in 1845.

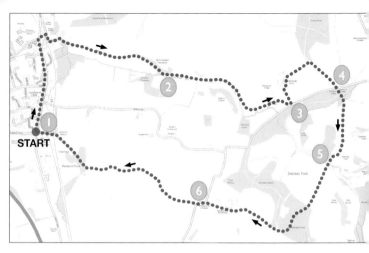

THE ROUTE

1. Take the High Street and Belmont Hill north to Water Lane on the right. Turn right and go under the railway arch. Keep straight on up the wide concrete access road, over the stream and passing right of the sewage works. Continue with the field to the right and the high ground to the left, to the marker post at the corner of the trees. Bear slight right, with the trees to the left, to the far corner.

2. Keep this direction through the trees, past the footbridge and keeping the Debden Water stream to the right. Carry on left of the telegraph pole with the hedge on your right, past a marker post close to some open ground. Follow the path left over a stile and continue to the stile at the end by the black wooden garage. Cross and turn right, down the driveway to the road.

3.   Turn sharp left up the farm driveway to the marker post on the right and turn right, going up the track parallel to the telegraph poles. At the corner of Howe Wood, bear right along the bridleway/farm track to the road.

4.   Keep this direction over the road and through the trees, continuing up the hill and over the concrete area (watch out for the concealed cattle grid). Follow the hardcore road, bearing right through the gap in the trees and over the bridge straddling the end of the lake.

5.   Carry on uphill into Cabbage Wood and follow the track through to the other side. Exit through the massive iron kissing gate and take the wide gritty farm road, past the buildings at Waldegraves to meet the road at a corner.

6.   Keep straight on, bearing slightly left and taking the farm road to the right/straight on. The path wanders past some trees, on the other side of which is a disused chalk quarry, and leads eventually down to the station. Cross the footbridge and follow Station Road ahead to the High Street and back to your starting point.

2. CASTLE HEDINGHAM

THE ESSENTIALS

Distance: 3¾ miles (6 km)

Route: Easy, several easy slopes, some stiles and gates

Time: Approx. 2 hours

Terrain: Hard paths, grassy fields, field edges and wider hardcore farm roads. A short section crosses a field which may be muddy in the wet

Starting Point: Falcon Square, Castle Hedingham. Grid ref TL784355, postcode CO9 3BY

Parking: Sensible roadside parking in the village

Food and Toilets: The Bell Inn, the Wheatsheaf Inn, the Old Moot House Restaurant and Buckley's Tea Rooms. No public toilets in the village

Maps: OS Explorer 195 (Braintree and Saffron Walden); OS Landranger 155 (Bury St Edmunds)

INTRODUCTION

Hedingham Castle is the ancestral seat of the de Vere family, Earls of Oxford, given by William I to Aubrey de Vere in 1086. The castle was completed by the middle of the twelfth century, although the keep is the only remaining part of the original structure. Several members of the de Vere family have left their mark on English history. The third Aubrey de Vere became the 1st Earl in 1141. The 11th Earl fought at the Battle of Agincourt, and his son John de Vere, the 12th Earl, took the Lancastrian side in the Wars of the Roses; both he and his elder son Aubrey were beheaded in 1462. John de Vere's second son, also John, became the 13th Earl and played a pivotal role in English history, providing military advice to Henry Tudor during the Battle of Bosworth Field.

A hundred years later Edward, the 17th Earl, had a reputation as a playwright and poet, and his name is among those suggested as the 'real' author of the works of Shakespeare. Another Aubrey, the 20th and last Earl, fought for the Royalists in the Civil War. He died with no male heir, and there were no other claimants to the title. However, it is classed as dormant rather than extinct, and the present owner of Hedingham Castle, Jason Lindsay, can trace his ancestry to the de Veres through both his parents.

Two blue plaques on houses in Castle Hedingham commemorate famous residents. Mark Catesby was born in the village in 1682. An avid student of natural history, in 1714 Catesby visited his sister in Virginia, returning in 1719 via the West Indies. He brought back a considerable collection of specimens and information and undertook a further expedition from 1722 to 1726, spending the rest of his life producing illustrations and a book, his *Natural History of Carolina, Florida and the Bahama Islands*.

The other plaque remembers Eric Ravilious, born in London in 1903. He was an artist and wood engraver who bought Bank House in Castle Hedingham in 1934 with his wife and fellow artist Tirzah Garwood. Ravilious worked mainly in watercolours, and at the start of World War II he became a war artist, producing some iconic work illustrating naval warfare during the first part of the war. In 1942 he visited an RAF station in Iceland where he joined a search party looking for a missing aeroplane; tragically his own aircraft was also lost.

2. CASTLE HEDINGHAM WALK

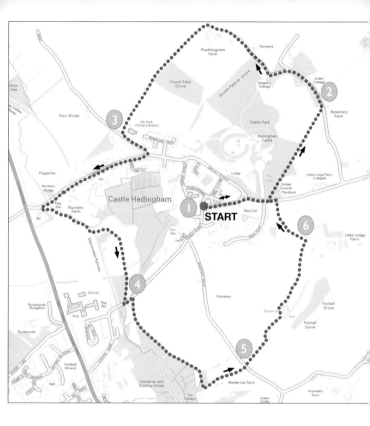

THE ROUTE

1. Follow Sudbury Road away from the village to the signpost at the '40' sign. Turn left up this enclosed path, through trees and along a field edge to reach Rosemary Lane.

2. Turn left and follow the lane to a marker post on the left. Bear left over the metal-railed footbridge and through the metal gate to the fence corner on the left. Bear further left

over the stile in the far corner. Keep ahead with the hedge and trees to the left through the corner. Keep this direction, with the hedge still left, to the road.

3. Go left to the T-junction, cross and take the roadside path to the right, heading down and over the bridge to the footpath signpost at the bus stop. Turn left along the path, with the River Colne to the left, to the marker post at the metal gate. Follow the path through the undergrowth with trees and hedge to the right, bearing right through a kissing gate. Continue through the trees, with the fence to the left, to the road.

4. Turn left over the bridge to the signpost. Take the path right, with the Colne now on the right. Carry on through the edge of the trees, bearing right at the end to a junction of tracks near a house. Take the wide driveway left with the fence and trees to the right, to the road.

5. Cross and pass the signpost, walking up the field edge with the dyke to the right. Keep on this track, left and right at the corners and left and right where the reservoir is hidden among the trees. The track continues up a slope, with the fence and hedge to the right, to a marker post.

6. Turn left past the tree and go straight on across the field to the hedge. Turn right along the field edge and take the path bearing left, through the hedge gap, down a slope through trees, past the barrier, down the steps and across the road to the roadside path. Turn left into the village and back to your starting point.

3. EAST MERSEA FLATS

THE ESSENTIALS

Distance: 3¼ miles (5¼ km)

Route: Mainly grass-topped embankments, grassy fields, hard paths, field edges and one section of not very busy road

Time: Approx. 1½ hours

Terrain: Easy, flat, some gates (no stiles)

Starting Point: Cudmore Grove Country Park, Bromans Lane, East Mersea. **Grid ref** TM 065146, **postcode** CO5 8UE

Parking: Pay and display at Cudmore Grove Country Park car park

Food and Toilets: The Dog and Pheasant and Mehalah's on East Road, the Company Shed on Coast Road, West Mersea. Public toilets at Cudmore Grove Country Park

Maps: OS Explorer 184 (Colchester); OS Landranger 168 (Colchester)

INTRODUCTION

Mersea Island, 12 miles from Colchester, is 5 miles (8 km) long, 2 miles (3.2 km) wide and about 8 square miles (25 square km) in area. It is divided very neatly into two areas – the larger, more commercialised West Mersea with its holiday homes, guest houses, shops and restaurants; and the smaller, quieter East Mersea, with its caravan and camp sites, Cudmore Grove Country Park and extensive mud flats teeming with wildlife.

The mud flats play host to a vast range of waders and water birds, resident and migrant, summer and winter. Brent geese always arrive in large numbers each winter. The low cliffs at the western end of Cudmore are being eroded year on year. As they disappear into the sea the fossilised bones of animals appear, having remained hidden for up to half a million years. Several skeletons of animals usually considered more at home on the African continent have been found in this area.

The pillbox near the car park is one of a line along the south-east coast of the island, part of the extensive fortifications constructed during the early part of World War II when the island was considered to be at risk of invasion. There were also searchlight systems, several observation posts and a battery of large-calibre ex-naval guns. Also on this shoreline are the earth ramparts of a fort built to protect the estuary in Tudor/Stuart times.

The Strood, the causeway linking the island with the mainland and carrying the B1025 road, is subject to frequent flooding at high tide and must not be crossed during these events. The oak piles used in its construction have been dated to the late seventh century by dendrochronologists.

The Romans in nearby Colchester (Camulodunum) used Mersea Island as a holiday destination. At least one high-ranking Roman official chose the island as his final resting place. A mound just off the road to East Mersea was excavated in 1912; the archaeologists found a lead-lined casket in which there was an urn containing cremated human remains.

3. EAST MERSEA FLATS WALK

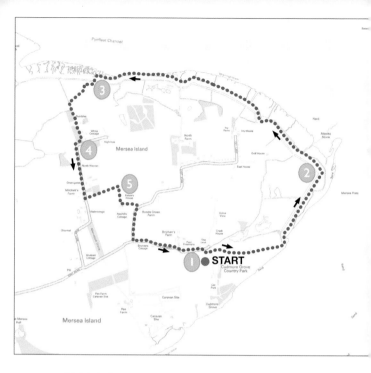

THE ROUTE

1. Walk out of the car park along the wide track mown into the grass, past the concrete pillbox to the path at the coastline and turn left past the East Mersea Flats signpost. Carry on along this rough tarmac path on the top of the embankment.

2. Follow the path left on a less substantial surface, past a large wooden building. Go through a metal kissing gate to the marker post and turn left down the uneven steps.

3. Go through the kissing gate at the dyke and bear right (there is normally a track in the grass) to a marker post at the boundary ahead. Turn left to the next marker post, go across the footbridge and turn left along the path through the trees. Continue up and down the steps and keep ahead on the wider driveway between trees to the T-junction of tracks.

4. Turn right and follow the road left. As the houses on the left end, turn left through the gate/gap, past the almost hidden signpost and along the field edge with the hedge to the left. Carry on between fields to the marker post at the hedge ahead.

5. Take the field edge right to the marker post in the corner, and turn left along the path between hedges and along the gravel drive to the road. Turn right and follow the road left, up to Broman's Lane. Turn left along this access road to the Country Park car park and your starting point.

4. EPPING FOREST

THE ESSENTIALS

Distance: 4 miles (6½ km)

Route: Easy, several easy slopes, one slightly steeper. No stiles, some gates

Time: Approx. 2 hours

Terrain: Hard and grassy woodland paths. The busy A104 road is crossed twice

Starting Point: The parking area at High Beech, Epping Forest. **Grid ref** TQ 411982, **postcode** IG10 4AE

Parking: Dedicated roadside parking, often very busy at weekends

Food and Toilets: The King's Oak pub adjacent to the car park; two snack bars, one in a caravan and one in a hut, in the parking area. Public toilets adjacent to parking area

Maps: OS Explorer 174 (Epping Forest and Lee Valley); OS Landranger 177 (East London)

INTRODUCTION

Epping Forest is a magical place to visit. It was known as Waltham Forest until the seventeenth century, having been developed by the Norman kings as a Royal Forest. This meant that although commoners could graze livestock and gather food and fuel, only the king could hunt there. The right to graze and gather fuel started to disappear during the early years of the nineteenth century; landowners started to enclose land for agriculture, and speculators began to develop land to house London's exploding population. The forest shrank at an alarming rate, but in 1871 the City of London started to prosecute landowners for illegal enclosure. This culminated in the Epping Forest Act through which the City bought 5,500 acres. Queen Victoria visited Chingford in 1882 and dedicated 'this beautiful forest to the use and enjoyment of my people for all time'. Commoners (people living within the forest) cannot now cut branches from trees for firewood, but they may graze cattle and still have the right to collect 'one faggot of dead or driftwood per day'.

Epping now consists of 6,118 acres of forest and heath in a narrow swathe of land 12 miles (19 km) south of Epping. It sits on a ridge between the rivers Roding and Lee, measuring only 2½ miles (4 km) at its maximum width. The land has been covered by trees since at least the late Stone Age and possibly longer. The Iron Age hillforts at Ambresbury Bank and Loughton Camp probably date back to about 500 BC.

Queen Elizabeth's Hunting Lodge near Chingford was built by Henry VIII in 1543 to enable him to watch hunting in progress when he was no longer able to follow on horseback. It was also used as a platform to shoot arrows at passing deer. The open sides were later filled in and it was then used first as a lodging for VIP huntsmen, and then as a gamekeeper's residence.

The highwayman Dick Turpin is alleged to have had a hiding place within the forest, as well as using its secluded byways to pursue his trade. The heavy tree cover, easy road access and proximity to London have made the forest a popular place to hide murder victims in fiction as well as fact. Charles Dickens, Dorothy L. Sayers and the TV programmes *EastEnders* and *New Tricks* have all used the forest as the setting for dark deeds.

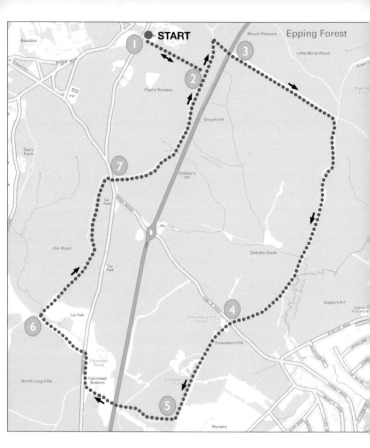

THE ROUTE

1. Facing the King's Oak pub, turn right for 75 yards up to the green gates on the right. Turn left along a faintly marked path, following parallel to the wooden fence on the left, to a junction with a more substantial path. Take note of this junction – it is not marked but you will need to recognise it on the return journey.

2. Take this track left to a triangular junction marked with a blue arrow marker post. Bear right down the track which leads to the A104.

3. Cross this busy road with great care. Go through the car park and bear right past a blue arrow marker post. Fork right and turn right at the next blue arrow, and go straight on past the final blue arrow; the track leads eventually to the road. Keep ahead, left of the first Strawberry Hill Pond and keep going, passing left of the second, larger pond to where the track bears right to a wider grassier track. (**Note**: Strawberry Hill Ponds are just two of the more than one hundred ponds and lakes within the forest. Most are man-made, having started life as gravel pits, while several are the result of World War II bombs and doodlebugs. All have been taken over by local wildlife and provide habitats for a wide range of species.)

4. Take this track right back to the A104, and again cross with care. Go through the narrow wooden gate and continue, bearing slight right on the substantial path to the tarmac-covered Fairmead Road.

5. Turn right to a white-topped post on the left; turn left along this wide clearing with the trees on the immediate left, to reach a junction with a more substantial track. Turn right.

6. Follow this track to the road and cross. Continue past the metal barrier opposite.

7. Keep on this track over the humps and through the dips to the unmarked junction at point 2, then turn left back to the road close to the King's Oak pub. Turn right, back to the car park.

5. HADLEIGH CASTLE

THE ESSENTIALS

Distance: 3 miles (5 km)

Route: Medium, a steep slope down and then back up again, no stiles, some gates

Time: Approx. 1½ hours

Terrain: Gritty tracks, grassy paths, hard paths and wider hardcore access roads

Starting Point: Hadleigh Country Park, Chapel Lane, Benfleet, Southend. **Grid ref** TQ 800869, **postcode** SS7 2PP

Alternative Starting Point: Hadleigh Farm, Castle Lane, Benfleet, Southend. **Grid ref** GR TQ 809864, **postcode** SS7 2AP

Parking: Pay and display parking at both starting locations

Food and Toilets: Salvation Army restaurants and public toilets at both starting locations

Maps: OS Explorer 175 (Southend-on-Sea and Basildon); OS Landranger 178 (Thames Estuary)

INTRODUCTION

Hadleigh Castle was built in the first half of the thirteenth century by Hubert de Bergh, Earl of Kent and the King's Justiciar. Hubert had ruled the kingdom during the minority of Henry III, who was only nine years old when he ascended the throne on the death of his father, King John, in 1216. At this time war with France was always more than a possibility, and Henry granted Hubert a licence to build a castle on the high, steep slopes north of the Thames Estuary. Unfortunately, however, Hubert did not choose his location well; the castle was built on an unstable hill of clay and has suffered from subsidence ever since.

Hubert enjoyed a prickly relationship with Henry, and on his death in 1243 Henry took ownership of the castle. The fortunes of the building ebbed and flowed, often reflecting the current state of relations with France. It also began to suffer damage as the land started to slide inexorably down the slope. From the beginning of the fifteenth century the importance of castles declined and by the middle of the sixteenth century the site was uninhabited and virtually derelict.

The ruins were sold to Sir Richard Rich, an avaricious Tudor courtier who made a profit on his purchase by selling any useable stone. The only stone remaining today is the rubble filling between the stronger outer walls. In 1891 the castle and surrounding land were bought by William Booth for the Salvation Army. He established a farm colony to train disadvantaged Londoners in agricultural and rural trades, with a view to them using their skills in overseas colonies. The centre continues to train people with special educational needs in the farm and rare breeds centre. There is also a tea room and farm shop. The castle itself was given to the Ministry of Works in 1948 and is now looked after by English Heritage.

The country park was first proposed in 1970, but did not open until 1987. It is now a Site of Special Scientific Interest containing woodland, scrub grassland, salt marsh and tidal flats, home to a range of mammals, birds, invertebrates and a considerable variety of flora. The 376-acre park is looked after by the Essex County Council Ranger Service. Hadleigh Farm and parts of the country park were the venue for the mountain biking events of the 2012 London Olympics.

5. HADLEIGH CASTLE WALK

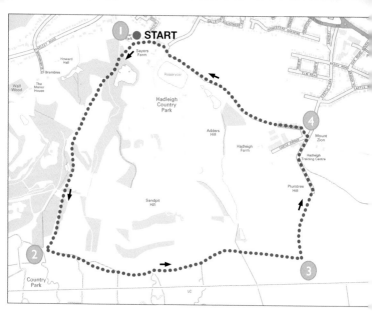

THE ROUTE

1. Take the path left of the play area and past both cattle grids. Keep on the lower path to the right, bearing left, with the trees to the right, over another cattle grid to a marker post marked 'PRIDE'. Turn right and zigzag down the gritty path, doubling back over the next cattle grid. Keep on this path through the green pinch barriers, across the track and through the wooden kissing gate. Follow the grass track ahead, downslope past the 'COURAGE' marker post and over the cattle grid.

2. Turn left along the track, with the fence and the hedge to the left. At a signpost the track joins the gritty path straight on

(this is a multi-use track) and carries on over a cattle grid. Keep this direction along a left-hand field edge with a hedge to the left and the field to the right. Reach the signpost on the left; there is a farm road on the right just a few yards further on.

3. Go through the green kissing gate on the left and take the hardcore farm road upslope, passing left of the castle entrance. Keep straight on past the signpost. At this point the end of Southend pier may be seen to the east. Bear right through the green pinch barriers to the signpost.

4. Turn left and bear right, then left past the front of the houses. Continue through the gap to the left of the barn ahead and follow the grit path pack to the starting point and the car park.

6. LAYER MARNEY TOWER

THE ESSENTIALS

Distance: 4½ miles (7¼ km)

Route: Easy, several easy slopes, two stiles and several gates

Time: Approx. 2¼ hours

Terrain: Grassy fields and farm roads, field edges and wider hardcore farm roads. There is also a section of road and some short pieces of cultivated field, which may be muddy in wet weather

Starting Point: An unsurfaced lay-by on a corner of the B1022, north-east of Tiptree. **Grid ref** TL 922187, **postcode** CO5 9XG

Alternative Starting Point: The Layer Marney Tower car park. **Grid ref** TL 928176, **postcode** CO5 9US

Parking: At both starting locations (the Tower car park is pay and display)

Food and Toilets: Refreshments at Layer Marney Tower or in Tiptree (2 miles away). No public toilets

Maps: OS Explorer 184 (Colchester);
OS Landranger 168 (Colchester)

INTRODUCTION

Henry, 1st Lord Marney was Henry VIII's Lord Privy Seal. He intended his new house, which he started to build around 1520, to rival the other great Tudor palace at Hampton Court. He saw only an impressive gatehouse, a brick-built church and some other ancillary buildings finished before he died in 1523. His son undertook to see the project through to completion but he also died only two years later, leaving no children

The tower was cleverly designed to make it seem bigger than it actually is. At first glance it appears to be eight stories high, but each floor has two windows, one on top of the other. It is not an optical illusion but a very effective trick on the subconscious. The building reflected the contemporary belief that the bigger, the more costly and flamboyant the house, the more important the owner. At 80 feet (24 metres) it is the tallest Tudor gatehouse in the country, with 99 steps to the top of the tower. Built of red brick mixed with black-glazed bricks in a form of decoration called diapering, there is further decoration made of terracotta. Although the crenellations are only decorative as the house was never meant to be a fortress, Marney still had to obtain special permission from the king to include them in his design.

The house has passed through many families in the intervening centuries, and witnessed many momentous events. On 22 April 1884 the Great Colchester Earthquake struck the area. Measuring around 4.6 on the Richter Scale and with an epicentre situated between Wivenhoe and Abberton, the earthquake caused massive damage to buildings in a wide area south and south-east of Colchester, and the church at Virley was almost totally destroyed. Layer Marney Tower was badly damaged and experts believed it was irreparable. Brother and sister Alfred and Kezia Peach took on the expensive job, which was continued by Walter de Zoete, who left the tower with an interior more Edwardian than Tudor.

Gerald and Susan Charrington fell in love with the tower after their marriage in the adjacent church in 1957. They bought the property in 1959 and it has remained in their family ever since. It is now a stunning venue for events and weddings, as well as being a family home.

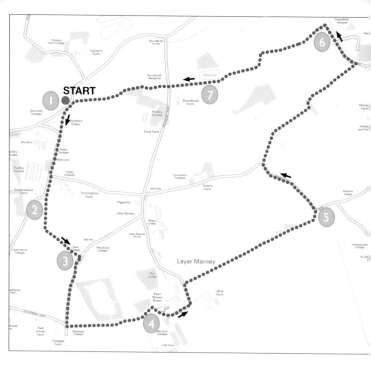

THE ROUTE

1. Facing the road, turn left along the verge to the hedge gap on the left before the bus stop. Turn left along the path in the grass to the road. Take the road left, past the junction to the small lay-by on the corner where the road swings right.

2. Cross the stile in the corner and continue down the fenced path and through the gap at the end. Bear left across this field to the signpost in the hedge gap. Cross the footbridge and continue to the road.

3. Take the road right to the junction and the signpost beyond. Turn left along the gravel drive and continue straight on up the field edge with the hedge to the left. As the field edge veers right, bear left across a footbridge. Carry on between the hedge and the fence to a three-way signpost.

4. Turn right, signposted to the church, and then left through the hedge gap into the churchyard. Pass to the right of the church and out of the gate. Turn left along the stony driveway to the road and turn left, up to the signpost on the right. Turn right up the path between fields. Go through the gap at the end and bear left to the road.

5. Turn left to the top where the road turns left, and go right through the gate. Cross the field diagonally to the track on the far side and turn right, keeping the hedge left, to the far left corner. Follow the track left and right and continue on the left-hand field edge, through the gap in the corner and along the path to the road. Turn left on the road, going through Birch Green to the footpath signpost at the end.

6. Take the gravel drive left, passing right of the houses and past a metal gate. Keep on this track around a double bend and slightly left at the reservoir to where the main track bears left at the far corner of the reservoir.

7. Go through the kissing gate on the right and keep your direction through more kissing gates and over the footbridge to the road. Cross and keep straight on, down steps and over the stile; carry on up the right-hand field edge between the hedge and the fence and over the stile footbridge in the corner. Turn left along the field edge, keeping the hedge to the left all the way to the road. The lay-by is to the left.

7. PAPER MILL LOCK

THE ESSENTIALS

Distance: 5½ miles (8.8 km)

Route: Grassy fields, field edges, riverbank and wider hardcore farm roads. There is also a section across a field which may be under cultivation and possibly muddy in wet weather

Time: Approx. 3 hours

Terrain: Easy, one easy slope down and back up, several stiles and gates

Starting Point: Crossroads near the General's Arms pub, The Ridge, Little Baddow. **Grid ref** TL 781072, postcode CM3 4SX

Parking: Sensible roadside parking in the village

Food and Toilets: The General's Arms and the Rodney Inn; tea room at the Paper Mill Lock. No public toilets

Maps: OS Explorer 183 (Chelmsford and the Rodings); OS Landranger 167 (Chelmsford)

INTRODUCTION

The River Chelmer at Paper Mill Lock has been canalised since the end of the eighteenth century. The river rises between Debden Green and Thaxted, flowing around the eastern side of Great Dunmow, then south-east and south to Chelmsford and a confluence with the River Can. The river turns east, where it becomes the Chelmer and Blackwater Navigation. The waterway continues east to join the Blackwater Estuary east of Maldon.

Plans to canalise the river were first promoted in 1677, but finance was always an issue. A plan passed in 1766 failed because money could not be raised in time. The town and port of Maldon normally opposed these plans on commercial grounds, but in the end an Act of Parliament authorising the work was passed. This solved the problem by going around Maldon to a new basin at Heybridge Port east of the town. The Chelmer and Blackwater Navigation, built between 1793 and 1797, runs from the centre of Chelmsford for 14 miles (22.5 km), descending 75 feet (23 metres) at Beeleigh, joining the River Blackwater and skirting the northern edge of Maldon.

Trade on the Navigation peaked at 60,000 tons of cargo per year in the middle of the nineteenth century – mainly coal going in and grain coming out. A wharf close to Paper Mill Lock handled cargo for Little Baddow. Two mills stood close to the lock when it was first built, one for grinding grain for bread, while more unusually the other ground chemicals for paper production.

The lock was often used as an overnight stop for the barge crews, who could bed down for the night in a bunkroom with their horses stabled in what is now the tearoom. The canal was not as badly affected as some by the coming of the railways, since there was never a direct railway connection between Chelmsford and Maldon. However, traffic and revenues declined through the first part of the twentieth century and the last commercial journey took place in 1972. Unusually, the canal is still owned by the original company because it was not nationalised with the rest of the canals in 1948. They allowed pleasure boats on the route after 1972, but were still unable to make the canal pay. The canal is now operated by the Inland Waterways Association, a charity that campaigns for the use, maintenance and restoration of all of Britain's inland waterways.

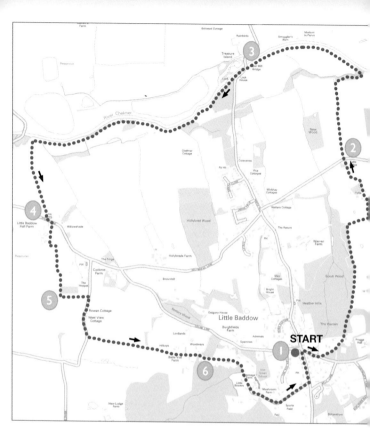

THE ROUTE

1. From the crossroads, go right into Spring Elms Lane to the signpost on the left. Take the gravel driveway bearing left of the white house. Go through the gap between the fence and the trees into Heather Hills Nature Reserve. Keep on the path and continue ahead at the signpost to the fence at the bottom. Turn right along the field edge and go through the

gap in the corner. Take the track left, passing right of the houses, and continue to the road.

2. Cross and keep ahead, between fields with the dyke to the left, to the trees. Turn right along the field edge, bearing left to the River Chelmer. Turn left along the riverbank to the road at Paper Mill Bridge. Cross this busy road carefully.

3. Go through the gate and keep on the path between the tearoom and Paper Mill Lock. Keep the river to your right, past the marker post on the left to a signpost just before a blue handrailed footbridge. Go through the gap and cross the field ahead up the slight slope, passing right of the church. Descend the steps to the road.

4. Turn left and walk to the signpost at the road entry on the right. Go past the stile and the marker disc, bearing left past the brick building to a junction at a telegraph pole. Keep left then right, past another telegraph pole. Continue on this farm road and then on the grass track between the fence and the hedge to an easily-missed gap in the hedge marked by a disc.

5. Turn left across this field and over a stile. Continue up the path to the road. Turn right past the white house to the signpost on the left; cross the stile and take the narrow path between the hedge and the fence. Continue through a metal kissing gate to a junction of wide tracks.

6. Turn right to a marker post with a double yellow arrow and take the narrow path left. Bear right at the junction and join a driveway ahead, bearing left to a tarmac surface and a marker post. Bear right and follow this driveway left to the road. Turn left along the road, past the General's Arms to the crossroads.

8. LOG CHURCH

THE ESSENTIALS

Distance: 4½ miles (7¼ km)

Route: Easy, some easy slopes, several stiles and gates

Time: Approx. 2¼ hours

Terrain: Grassy fields, roadside paths, field edges and wider hardcore farm roads

Starting Point: Car park close to the library in Chipping Ongar. **Grid ref TL 552031, postcode CM5 9AR**

Parking: In the car park at the start point

Food and Toilets: Restaurants, cafés, pubs and takeaways close by in Chipping Ongar. Public toilets adjacent to car park

Maps: OS Explorer 183 (Chelmsford and the Rodings); OS Landranger 167 (Chelmsford)

INTRODUCTION

Sted or *stead* is an Old English word meaning place, so Greensted literally means 'green place'. The name of the village has been shortened in recent years from the more difficult Greensted-juxta-Ongar, which was originally used to differentiate the village from the other Greenstead in Essex. The *juxta* comes from 'juxtapose' (put next to), a word which itself seems to be used very little today, with the Ongar coming from the nearby town of Chipping Ongar.

St Andrew's in Greensted is a church built from split logs, and for many years it was believed to be the oldest wooden church in the world, and possibly the oldest wooden building in Europe. As with many older buildings it is difficult to be exact about age, but Greensted is thought to have been the site of a holy building for as long as there has been Christianity in England. While archaeologists were investigating the church in the 1960s they discovered evidence of timber buildings predating the present church. These experts originally identified the logs as having been cut in the middle of the ninth century, although more modern dating methods have fixed the date at the middle of the eleventh century.

The nave, the oldest part of the church, is built in a traditional Saxon style with split oak tree trunks. This style makes the building a palisade church. The logs are piled into the ground or attached to a sill foundation, with the rounded edge facing the outside. These logs were load bearing and the roof was built on top of them. The church has been the subject of a constant process of rebuilding and updating ever since. The chancel, originally built in the same manner as the main church, was replaced by a brick structure in the sixteenth century, and the spire-topped tower was added during the seventeenth century. The Victorians seemed unable to resist rebuilding churches whether they needed it or not, and they reroofed the building and put in six dormer windows in place of the original three. They also rebuilt the porch.

In 1972, as part of a series celebrating British architecture, the Post Office issued a set of stamps illustrating five iconic churches. The lowest 3p denomination (3p to post a letter?) showed a painting of St Andrew's Church.

8. LOG CHURCH WALK

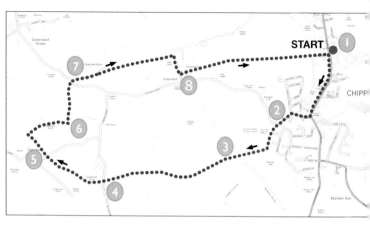

THE ROUTE

1. Turn right onto the High Street, through town to the junction
    with the Borough. Cross to the opposite pavement and turn
    right past the Two Brewers, bearing left up Greensted Road
    to the first footpath signpost.

2. Bear left up this hardcore track with the school to the right,
    continuing between trees to the marker post on the right.
    Bear right, parallel with the power lines over the field. Cross
    the footbridge in the hedge gap.

3. Continue up the left-hand field edge with the trees and dyke
    to the left. The path passes right of two small ponds and
    bears right at a marker post, with the trees and dyke still
    left. Cross the footbridge at the end. Continue along the
    right-hand field edge with the trees and hedge now on the
    right, over the two-sleeper bridge in the corner. Take the
    footpath slightly left, to the left of the tree, and go through
    the trees to the road.

4. Continue through the gate opposite, down the fenced path and turn right to the stile. Cross and bear right, through the boundary at the corner and up the field edge with the trees to the right. Follow the edge to the yellow-topped marker post and take the path right, through trees to the road.

5. Turn left and immediately right, between the hedge and fence to a yellow-topped post at the end. Turn right across the field to another post at a narrow metal gate, then follow the track through trees. At the next metal gate turn right on a wider path. At the marker post, turn left through a wooden kissing gate.

6. Continue through pinch stiles onto the enclosed path which leads through a kissing gate to the field edge. Turn right with the hedge to the right, and continue to the road.

7. Cross and follow the field edge, bearing slightly right to the footbridge at the end. Cross and walk up the concrete driveway to the Log Church.

8. After looking at the church, go through the churchyard gate and turn left. Take the wide tarmac drive to the left and go through the gate at the end, walking down the left-hand field edge with trees to the left. Continue over the footbridge and up the path between fields, straight on up the road into Chipping Ongar and back to the car park.

9. STOUR ESTUARY

INTRODUCTION

The source of the River Stour is close to the villages of Weston Colville, Weston Green and West Wratting in Cambridgeshire (south of Newmarket). It flows east and south-east past Haverhill and Sudbury, then through Constable Country – Dedham Vale, an Area of Outstanding Natural Beauty. For most of its course it forms the border between Suffolk and Essex, entering the wide Stour Estuary at Manningtree and flowing to its mouth at Harwich, where it is briefly joined by the River Orwell.

A joint stock company was set up in 1705 to make the river navigable from Sudbury to Manningtree. It raised £4,800 to 'cut and manage' the river. Lighters (unpowered barges) were still being used on the navigation until World War II. The River Stour Trust was formed in 1968 with the intention of reopening the waterway between Sudbury and the sea. The trust has successfully restored locks further up the river, but the limit of navigation for ships is still at Manningtree.

The estuary is a haven for various species of wildlife, particularly ducks and geese. An increasingly common bird is the little egret, a member of the heron family, snowy white in colour and slightly smaller than a grey heron. The bird was a very rare visitor to England until this century.

Manningtree claims to be the smallest town in England, covering only 47 acres (19 hectares), although there are towns with a smaller population. A notorious citizen of the town was Matthew Hopkins, who gained a reputation as England's Witchfinder General between 1644 and 1647. Without much authority Hopkins and his associate John Stearne travelled through East Anglia denouncing women as witches. The women found it very hard to defend themselves, as 'justice' and 'evidence' weighed very heavily against them. The two men presided over the prosecution and execution of some three hundred women. During this three-year period they were responsible for more judicial deaths for witchcraft than in the preceding hundred years. Every time they visited a town they were paid around twenty pounds, quite a fortune at the time and a good enough reason to find witches among a few innocent women.

Note: see p42 for a short extension to this walk to take in the beautiful Flatford Mill, the subject of some of Constable's most famous paintings.

9. STOUR ESTUARY WALK

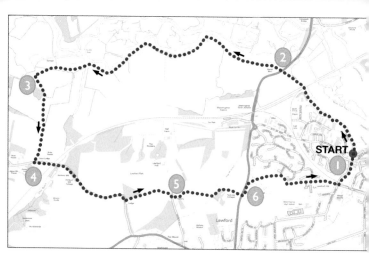

THE ROUTE

1. Climb to the top of the embankment at the back of the car park and turn left with the estuary to the right. As the main track appears to turn left, keep ahead on a slightly lower path between two sets of steps. Continue under the railway and up to the busy A137.

2. Cross with care and take the path past the signpost and litter bin. Continue with the river to the right. The path eventually comes to a junction at a metal kissing gate next to a National Trust sign and a long, low concrete structure to the right. Keep straight on with the hedge and trees to the left, to the wide hedge gap on the left.

3. Turn left across the concrete bridge and take the path ahead to the metal gate in the hedge ahead. Go through, cross the footbridge and bear left through the gates/footbridge at the

far left. Turn left through the wide gap and right, upslope between trees, passing right of the house to the road.

4. Take the road left under the railway. Continue up round a sharp right-hand bend to the signpost on the left. Turn left through the wooden gate, along the gravel drive between trees with the hedge to the left, to the wooden kissing gate on the right. Go through and bear left, through the next wooden gate to the signpost near the church.

5. Turn right and immediate left at the signpost next to the brick cottage. Go through a wide gateway and continue with the churchyard wall to the left, to the marker post on the right. Follow the track right into the dip, and bear left over Wignall Brook to the kissing gate. Bear right, upslope through a metal kissing gate. Continue left of the houses and to the A137.

6. Cross carefully and turn left on the roadside path to the signpost where the path ends. Turn right through the gap and bear right with the path along the bottom of the slope. Go right at the marker post. The track heads uphill, across the end of a tarmac path and behind the houses; follow the path right and left as it leads eventually to the road. Turn left, over the railway and down to the T-junction. Cross and continue up the path to the car park ahead.

9. STOUR ESTUARY WALK

THE FLATFORD MILL SPUR

It seems a pity not to include Flatford Mill in this walk, although it means venturing into Suffolk. It increases the route by a mile but adds another dimension to the walk, and you can easily make a day of it by the time you have wandered around the village. The mill, the watermill at Dedham just upstream and two local windmills were owned by the artist John Constable's father. The Dedham mill was replaced in Victorian times by the brick building, now converted into flats.

Flatford Mill features in several of Constable's paintings. *The Haywain*, showing a cart or wain being pulled across the river with the nearby Willy Lott's Cottage to one side, was painted from the front of the mill. *Flatford Mill (Scene on a Navigable River)*, completed in 1816, shows a young boy on a horse which is towing a lighter up the river, with the mill in the middle background. The mill, Willy Lott's Cottage and Bridge Cottage are all looked after by the National Trust, but are not open to the public. Willy Lott was a friend of Constable's who never ventured far from his home, in which he had been born. He complained of poor health and had the land that he owned worked by other people, and then lived frugally on the profits.

The Haywain was probably Constable's most famous painting, completed in 1821 and originally called *Landscape: Noon*. It made no immediate impression on the British art world when it was exhibited at the Royal Academy that year, but it was later exhibited at the 1824 Paris Salon where it won a gold medal. It then passed into private ownership before being acquired by the National Gallery in 1886. Most commonly seen as a fairly small domestic print, the original creates quite an impression at over six feet wide and four feet high.

To take the Flatford Mill spur, follow these instructions from the start of the Stour Estuary walk:

1. Climb to the top of the embankment at the back of the car park and turn left with the estuary to the right. As the main track appears to turn left, keep ahead on a slightly lower path between two sets of steps. Continue under the railway and up to the busy A137.

2. Cross with care and take the path past the signpost and litter bin. Continue with the river to the right. The path eventually comes to a junction at a metal kissing gate next to a National Trust sign and a long, low concrete structure to the right.

At this point, follow these instructions:

2a. At the junction on the other side of the kissing gate, at the National Trust sign, bear right along the path, keeping the long, low concrete structure to your right. The path leads to Flatford Mill, half a mile away.

After your visit to Flatford Mill, retrace your steps back to the junction by the National Trust sign and continue with the Stour Estuary walk instructions where you left off.

10. THAXTED

INTRODUCTION

Thaxted is a town with a sense of the Middle Ages. The church of St John the Baptist, St Mary and St Laurence is mainly late medieval, but it was not fully completed until the beginning of the sixteenth century. Its distinctive flying-buttressed spire dominates the town. It is one of the largest churches in Essex and some locals claim that it should be the county's cathedral.

The town's windmill, built in 1804, only worked for just over a century. It failed to find a buyer at auction in 1907, and gradually descended into dereliction. Restoration began in the 1970s, and over £100,000 has now been spent on the building and the machinery inside. The mill is open in the summer on weekend and bank holiday afternoons.

Gustav Holst, the composer of *The Planets* orchestral suite, lived in the house on Town Street marked by a blue plaque. He was born Gustavus von Holst in Cheltenham, dropping the 'von' from his name during World War I, as did most people with German-sounding names. He befriended Conrad Noel, Thaxted's vicar and something of a socialist firebrand, and became a pillar of the church, where he sometimes played the organ and acted as choirmaster. *The Planets*, his most popular composition, was written between 1914 and 1916. The Earth is not included as the music reflects his interest in astrology rather than astronomy. It was not performed until 29 September 1918, in the closing weeks of World War I. Holst did not believe it to be his best work, and complained bitterly that the suite's popularity eclipsed all his other work.

The early history of Thaxted's guildhall is not clear; tree-ring dating technology puts the date of construction at around 1460–70, refuting earlier theories that the building was mid-fourteenth century. Thaxted was a centre for the manufacture of cutlery during the early Middle Ages, and it had been thought that the building was the guildhall for the cutlers. This now seems unlikely, and it is believed that it may have been built simply as a meeting place. The hall had fallen into disrepair by the end of the seventeenth century, when it was restored by a local charity and used as a school until 1878. The building is now used for civic meetings and exhibitions throughout the year.

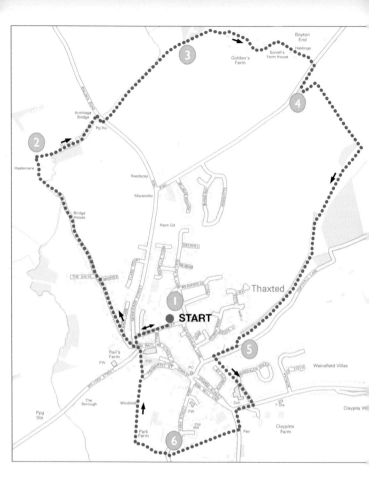

THE ROUTE

1. From the car park entrance, turn right. Turn left into Bell Lane and then turn right up Watling Street, passing right of the church. At the junction with Newbiggen Street, keep straight on along Watling Street, bearing right between houses. Continue between hedges out into the countryside, over the concrete bridge, left of the house to the marker post on the right.

2. Go through the hedge gap and turn right along the field edge with the hedge to the right, bearing left to the road. Turn right, across the stream and left down the driveway to Goddard's Farm. At the marker post take the path left, with stream and trees to the left, to a marker post on the left. Keep right/ straight on across the field to a junction of several farm roads.

3. Keep straight on/right up the stony farm track, and bear right with the hedge and left into the corner. Bear left through trees to a driveway, and continue right of the houses. Continue to the road and turn right along the verge to the signpost on the left.

4. Turn left past the metal barrier, and left over the footbridge. Continue along the right-hand field edge to the corner, and follow the edge of this narrow field to the bottom. Cross the footbridge and turn right along the field edge with trees to the right, bearing left through the right-hand corner. Keep on this field edge to a marker post. Descend the steps to the left and cross both footbridges. Go up the other side and turn right along the field edge with the hedge to the right. Exit at the far-left corner of the grassy area.

continued overpage

10. THAXTED WALK

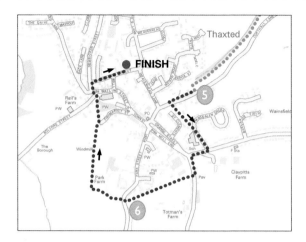

5. Turn right, down to the metal half-barriers on the left (no signpost or marker post here) and turn left between walls, passing left of the school and down to the road. Turn right to the B184 and cross to the roadside path, turning left towards Dunmow to the footpath signpost on the right. Turn right along this hedged path down to the B1051.

6. Turn right and immediate left, past the footpath signpost, up towards Park Farm and the Stables. Follow the track right to the junction and left to the top of the rise. Take the field edge right along the track with the hedge to the right, passing right of the windmill and left of the church back to Watling Street. Turn right then left along Bell Lane, then right at the end and back to the car park.